The Star-Spangled Banner

Introducing Primary Sources

by Tamra B. Orr

CAPSTONE PRESS
a capstone imprint

Little Explorer is published by Capstone Press,
1710 Roe Crest Drive, North Mankato, Minnesota 56003
www.mycapstone.com

The name of the Smithsonian Institution and the sunburst logo are registered trademarks of the
Smithsonian Institution. For more information, please visit www.si.edu.

Library of Congress Cataloging-in-Publication Data
Orr, Tamra.
The Star-spangled banner : introducing primary sources / by Tamra B. Orr.
pages cm. — (Smithsonian little explorer. Introducing primary sources.)
Includes index.
Summary: "Introduces young readers to primary sources related to the Star-Spangled Banner"—
Provided by publisher.
ISBN 978-1-4914-8226-1 (library binding)
ISBN 978-1-4914-8610-8 (paperback)
ISBN 978-1-4914-8616-0 (eBook PDF)
1. Baltimore, Battle of, Baltimore, Md., 1814—Juvenile literature. 2. Star-spangled banner (Song)—
Juvenile literature. 3. Key, Francis Scott, 1779–1843—Juvenile literature. 4. United States—History—
War of 1812—Flags—Juvenile literature. 5. Flags—United States—History—19th century—Juvenile
literature. I. Title.
E356.B2O77 2016
929.9'20973—dc23   2015030754

Editorial Credits
Michelle Hasselius, editor; Richard Parker, designer; Wanda Winch, media researcher;
Steve Walker, production specialist

Our very special thanks to Jennifer L. Jones, Chair, Armed Forces Division at the National Museum
of American History, Kenneth E. Behring Center, Smithsonian, for her curatorial review. Capstone
would also like to thank Kealy Gordan, Product Development Manager, and the following at
Smithsonian Enterprises: Ellen Nanney, Licensing Manager; Brigid Ferraro, Vice President, Education
and Consumer Products; Carol LeBlanc, Senior Vice President, Education and Consumer Products.

Photo Credits
Corbis: Bettmann, 19 (bottom); Courtesy of Lowell Moorhead, 17 (top), 29; Courtesy of Smithsonian
Institution: National Museum of American History, cover (top left); Getty Images: George Rose, 24,
Hulton Archive, 16 (left), 23 (bottom), MLB Photos/Mark Cunningham, 25 (bottom), WireImage/
KMazur, 25 (top); Granger, NYC, 4; Library of Congress, 23 (top), Music Division/Notated Music,
cover (bottom), 11 (left), 18, 21, Performing Arts Encyclopedia, 5, Prints and Photographs Division,
cover (top right), 6 (all), 7, 9 (right), 10, 12, 14, 15, 17 (bottom), 19 (top), 22, 28; Photo by Greg Pease,
courtesy of the Friends of Fort McHenry, 26; Ripley Entertainment Inc., 20; Shutterstock: Arevik, paper
design, Ismagilov, 9 (left); U.S. Army: Lt. Adrian C. Duff, 16 (right); U.S. Navy Media Content Services:
Petty Officer 2nd Class Joshua Wahl, 27 (top), Lt. j.g. Bobbie A. Camp, 27 (bottom); Wikimedia: George
Henry Preble, 8; J. Hill, 11 (right), Neutrality, 13

Printed in the United States of America in North Mankato, Minnesota.
009221CGS16

Table of Contents

Reaching Back to the Past

Have you ever wished you lived in a different time? Imagine traveling in a canoe with Lewis and Clark. Picture yourself sitting next to Benjamin Franklin at Independence Hall. One way to visit the past is through primary sources. Primary sources are made at the time of an event.

a wood carving made in 1885 of Francis Scott Key and the Star-Spangled Banner flag

Primary sources could be objects, photos, paintings, or newspaper articles. They can even be songs, such as "The Star-Spangled Banner."

"The Star-Spangled Banner" at a Glance

- written by Francis Scott Key
- originally titled "Defence of Fort M'Henry"
- inspired by the Battle of Baltimore during the War of 1812
- played at a baseball game for the first time in 1862
- became the official national anthem in 1931

DEFENCE OF FORT M'HENRY.

The annexed song was composed under the following circumstances—A gentleman had left Baltimore, in a flag of truce for the purpose of getting released from the British fleet, a friend of his who had been captured at Marlborough.—He went as far as the mouth of the Patuxent, and was not permitted to return lest the intended attack on Baltimore should be disclosed. He was therefore brought up the Bay to the mouth of the Patapsco, where the flag vessel was kept under the guns of a frigate, which he was compelled to witness the bombardment of Fort M'Henry, which the Admiral had boasted that he would carry in a few hours, and that the city must fall. He watched the flag at the Fort through the whole day with an anxiety that can be better felt than described, until the night prevented him from seeing it. In the night he watched the Bomb Shells, and at early dawn his eye was again greeted by the proudly waving flag of his country.

*Tune—*ANACREON IN HEAVEN.

O! say can you see by the dawn's early light,
 What so proudly we hailed at the twilight's last gleaming,
Whose broad stripes and bright stars through the perilous fight,
 O'er the ramparts we watch'd, were so gallantly streaming?
And the Rockets' red glare, the Bombs bursting in air,
Gave proof through the night that our Flag was still there;
 O! say does that star-spangled Banner yet wave,
 O'er the Land of the free, and the home of the brave?

On the shore dimly seen through the mists of the deep,
 Where the foe's haughty host in dread silence reposes,
What is that which the breeze, o'er the towering steep,
 As it fitfully blows, half conceals, half discloses?
Now it catches the gleam of the morning's first beam,
In full glory reflected now shines in the stream,
 'Tis the star spangled banner, O! long may it wave
 O'er the land of the free and the home of the brave.

And where is that band who so vauntingly swore
 That the havoc of war and the battle's confusion,
A home and a country, shall leave us no more?
 Their blood has washed out their foul footsteps pollution.
No refuge could save the hireling and slave,
From the terror of flight or the gloom of the grave,
 And the star-spangled banner in triumph doth wave,
 O'er the Land of the Free, and the Home of the Brave.

O! thus be it ever when freemen shall stand,
 Between their lov'd home, and the war's desolation,
Blest with vict'ry and peace, may the Heav'n rescued land,
 Praise the Power that hath made and preserv'd us a nation!
Then conquer we must, when our cause it is just,
And this be our motto—" In God is our Trust;"
 And the star-spangled banner in triumph shall wave,
 O'er the Land of the Free, and the Home of the Brave.

first known printing of Key's poem, "Defence of Fort M'Henry"

The Bombs Bursting in Air

On September 13, 1814, Francis Scott Key watched helplessly as the British Army attacked Fort McHenry in Baltimore, Maryland.

In this painting from 1913, Key watches the Battle of Baltimore from a British ship.

FACT

James Madison was U.S. president during the War of 1812 (1812–1815). He served as president from 1809 until 1817.

a portrait of President James Madison

During the War of 1812 (1812–1815), Key was a lawyer. The British Army had arrested an American doctor in Maryland. The doctor was being held on a British ship. Key traveled to Baltimore to try to get the doctor released. The two men were on the ship when Fort McHenry was attacked.

a 1905 painting of the attack on Fort McHenry in 1814

For 25 hours British soldiers bombed the American fort. Key was afraid the British Army had won the battle.

"It seemed as though mother earth had opened and was vomiting shot and shell in a sheet of fire and brimstone."
—Francis Scott Key

"Defence of Fort M'Henry"

As the sun rose, Key looked for the British flag flying over the fort. This would mean the British Army had won the battle. Instead Key saw the American flag.

1873 photo of the Star-Spangled Banner flag that flew over Fort McHenry in 1814

When Key saw the American flag, he grabbed a pencil and began writing. He wrote a poem called "Defence of Fort M'Henry." This poem would later be called "The Star-Spangled Banner." Key had no idea it would be sung all over the country years later.

Union Jack flag

FACT

Great Britain's flag is called the Union Jack. It is made up of flags from England, Scotland, and Ireland.

9

From Poem to Song

In 1814 a musician put Key's poem to music. The melody was from a British song written 40 years earlier.

In this photo from the mid-1900s, children from St. Rica's School in Cincinnati, Ohio, perform "The Star-Spangled Banner" using sign language.

Soon other songwriters were making small changes to the song's melody. They didn't want it to sound like the British song. Songwriters changed the speed of the song. They sang the lyrics much slower.

"The Star-Spangled Banner" sheet music from 1814

sheet music for "Twinkle, Twinkle Little Star"

A Closer Look at the Lyrics

Many people know the words to "The Star-Spangled Banner." But most don't know that Key wrote four verses, not just one. Each verse ends with the sentence, "O'er the land of the free and the home of the brave!"

Francis Scott Key's handwritten verses for what would become "The Star-Spangled Banner"

WHAT DOES IT MEAN?

Oh say, can you see, by the dawn's early light,
meaning: Could you see the American flag when the sun came up?

What so proudly we hail'd at the twilight's last gleaming?
meaning: We proudly saw the flag before dawn.

Whose broad stripes and bright stars, thro' the perilous fight,
meaning: The American flag's stars and stripes could be seen during the Battle of Baltimore.

O'er the ramparts we watch'd, were so gallantly streaming?
meaning: We looked over the fort to see the flag waving.

And the rockets' red glare, the bombs bursting in air,
meaning: The rockets and cannon fire from the British ship and Fort McHenry flew in the air.

Gave proof thro' the night that our flag was still there.
meaning: The cannon fire gave enough light to see the American flag was still flying over Fort McHenry.

O say, does that star-spangled banner yet wave? O'er the land of the free and the home of the brave?
meaning: Is the American flag still waving over the United States of America?

601 PENNSYLVANIA AVENUE

This plaque in Washington, D.C., marks the place where "The Star-Spangled Banner" was publicly sung for the first time.

An American Symbol

The Civil War (1861–1865) tore apart the United States in many ways. Soldiers often fought against people they knew.

a photo of the 36th Pennsylvania Infantry camp during the Civil War

During this war Key's song and the American flag meant more than ever. They reminded soldiers of the justice that they were fighting for. Others saw them as promises of freedom. When the war ended, the U.S. flag and "The Star-Spangled Banner" helped bring the country back together.

a photo of a Civil War soldier from the 37th Pennsylvania Infantry holding a flag

Supporting the War

In 1915 "The Star-Spangled Banner" was used to help raise money during World War I (1914–1918). President Woodrow Wilson's daughter Margaret recorded the song. People could buy the record for $1. Twenty-five cents from each sale was sent to the Red Cross to support the war effort.

a 1918 photo of American troops in France during World War I

a photo of German soldiers in 1918

a record of Margaret Wilson's version of "The Star-Spangled Banner"

a photo of Margaret Wilson in 1917

"The Star-Spangled Banner" was a popular song. In 1889 the U.S. Navy started playing the song each time they raised the U.S. flag. Soon the U.S. Army did the same.

"The Star-Spangled Banner" sheet music used by military bands in 1918

a photo of President Wilson throwing the first ball at a baseball game in 1916

In 1916 President Wilson ordered the song to be played at all military ceremonies. Two years later it was played during the World Series. The crowd loved it. A new tradition began.

FACT

At the 1918 World Series, "The Star-Spangled Banner" was played during the seventh inning. The Red Sox and the Cubs stopped playing. They placed their hands over their hearts during the song.

a photo of the fourth game of the 1918 World Series

An Anthem for the Nation

People loved "The Star-Spangled Banner" song. It made Americans think about the country. But it wasn't officially the national anthem. The United States did not have one.

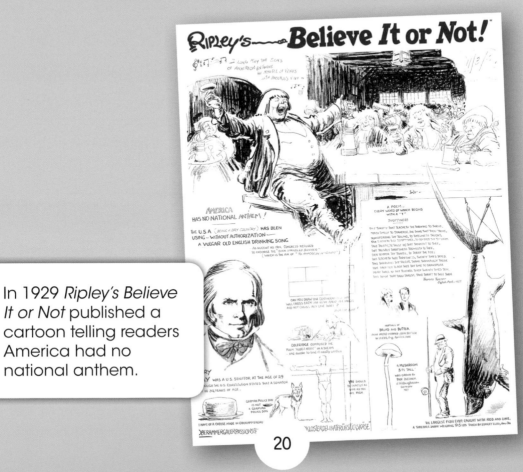

In 1929 *Ripley's Believe It or Not* published a cartoon telling readers America had no national anthem.

Almost the National Anthem

There were other songs in the running for America's national anthem.

"Yankee Doodle," America's unofficial national anthem after the Revolutionary War

"America the Beautiful," by Katharine Lee Bates

"Hail Columbia," by Joseph Hopkinson and Philip Phile

"My Country, 'Tis of Thee," by Reverend Samuel Francis Smith

"The Battle Hymn of the Republic," by Julia Ward Howe

The problem was deciding which song to choose. In 1928 a song-writing contest was held. More than 4,500 people submitted songs. But none of the songs were chosen.

sheet music from 1854 of "Yankee Doodle" and "Hail Columbia"

People wrote letters and signed petitions to make "The Star-Spangled Banner" the national anthem. Finally on March 3, 1931, President Herbert Hoover signed the bill into law. This officially made "The Star-Spangled Banner" America's anthem.

portrait of President Herbert Hoover

a copy of the 1931 law that made "The Star-Spangled Banner" America's national anthem

1508   SEVENTY-FIRST CONGRESS. Sess. III. Chs. 436, 437. 1931.

March 3, 1931.
[H. R. 14.]
[Public, No. 823.]

CHAP. 436.—An Act To make The Star-Spangled Banner the national anthem of the United States of America.

The Star-Spangled Banner.
Composition known as, designated the national anthem.

Be it enacted by the Senate and House of Representatives of the United States of America in Congress assembled, That the composition consisting of the words and music known as The Star-Spangled Banner is designated the national anthem of the United States of America.

Approved, March 3, 1931.

Not everyone was happy "The Star-Spangled Banner" was chosen. Many people thought the song was too hard to sing. Some notes are very high. Even the best singers have trouble reaching them.

Kate Smith, shown here in 1945, recorded a version of "The Star-Spangled Banner" that was an instant hit.

FACT

Even today some people would like the national anthem to change. They want a song that is easier to sing.

New Voices

Years after Francis Scott Key wrote "The Star-Spangled Banner," his words are still sung. The national anthem is played at the beginning of many sporting events, including the Super Bowl and the World Series.

a photo of Whitney Houston singing the national anthem at the Super Bowl in 1991

24

Many performers have sung the national anthem during sporting events.

Beyoncé sang the anthem at the Super Bowl in 2004.

José Feliciano sang the anthem at the Major League Baseball All-Star Game in 2010.

Happy Birthday

In September 2014 our national anthem turned 200 years old. People in Baltimore celebrated in many ways. Music played. Fireworks exploded in the air. The U.S. Navy's Blue Angels shot across the sky. People will continue to treasure our national anthem for years to come.

students formed a giant U.S. flag to celebrate the 200th anniversary of the national anthem at Fort McHenry

a naval petty officer sings the national anthem before a baseball game in 2009

a photo of the Blue Angels flying in a diamond pattern at the Naval Air Station Oceana Air Show in 2014

FACT

The Blue Angels are the U.S. Navy's flying aerobatic team. They are known for their high speeds and tricks in the air.

Timeline

June 18, 1812   U.S. declares war against
Great Britain; the War
of 1812 begins

September 1814   British Army attacks Fort
McHenry; Francis Scott Key
writes a poem later called
"The Star-Spangled Banner"

1814   Key's poem is turned into a song

1862   "The Star-Spangled Banner" is played
at the first baseball game

1889   U.S. Navy plays "The Star-Spangled
Banner" each time they raise the U.S. flag

1915   Margaret Wilson sings "The Star-Spangled Banner" to raise money for the Red Cross during World War I

1916   President Wilson orders the song to be played at all military ceremonies

1928   a song-writing contest is held to pick America's national anthem

March 3, 1931   "The Star-Spangled Banner" officially becomes the country's national anthem

September 2014   "The Star-Spangled Banner" turns 200 years old

Glossary

anthem—a song identified with a group or cause

banner—a long piece of material with writing, pictures, or designs on it;
a banner is hung from a pole or displayed at a sporting event or parade

battle—a fight between two military groups

bill—a written plan for a new law

ceremony—special actions, words, or music performed for a special event

lyrics—the words of a song

melody—a tune

petition—a letter signed by many people telling leaders how signers feel
about a certain issue or situation

primary source—an original document

record—a disk with grooves on which sound, especially music, is played

spangle—a bright decoration

Super Bowl—the championship football game between the winners of the
National Football Conference and the American Football Conference

tradition—a custom, idea, or belief passed down through time

verse—one part of a poem or song; a verse is made up of several lines

World Series—the championship baseball game between the winners of the
American League and the National League

Read More

Gaspar, Joe. *The National Anthem. American Symbols.* New York: PowerKids Press, 2014.

Kulling, Monica. *Francis Scott Key's Star-Spangled Banner.* Step into Reading. New York: Random House Children's Books, 2012.

Monroe, Tyler. *The Star-Spangled Banner.* U.S. Symbols. North Mankato, Minn.: Capstone Press, 2014.

Internet Sites

FactHound offers a safe, fun way to find Internet sites related to this book. All of the sites on FactHound have been researched by our staff.

Here's all you do:

Visit *www.facthound.com*

Type in this code: 9781491482261

 Check out projects, games and lots more at
www.capstonekids.com

Critical Thinking Using the Common Core

1. What event caused Francis Scott Key to write what would later be called "The Star-Spangled Banner?" Use the text to help you with your answer. (Key Ideas and Details)

2. "The Star-Spangled Banner" has four verses. What is a verse? (Craft and Structure)

3. Look at the photo on page 24. What is happening in the picture? (Integration of Knowledge and Ideas)

Index